STAMFORD
350 Years
1641–1991

STAMFORD

350 Years

1641–1991

Robert Atwan
Consulting Editor

Kenneth H. Brief
Consulting Editor

Barry Hoffman
Editor

William Hubbell
Photographer

Renee Kahn
Historical Consultant

PUBLISHED BY

THE ADVOCATE
AND
THE FERGUSON LIBRARY

anniversary (our 38th in Stamford) my wife and I mused not without a sense of loss that in all those years we had not dined away from our own house on weekends more often than 8 or 10 times. Stamford has been the place to go home to.

That of course is the exception imposed by the hard requirements of a certain kind of professional life. The social life within Stamford is vigorously pursued. We have a young neighbor, and if ever I drove by his house on a weekend to find there fewer than eight cars, I would conclude that he had contracted typhoid. The Yacht Club is oversubscribed, and of course there are golf clubs and tennis clubs, fraternal, ethnic, and religious social centers. The political life of the city, as readers of the history that follows will be reminded, revolved to a considerable extent during the past few decades on the question of urban renewal, with those in favor prevailing over those opposed. My relative ignorance of Stamford politics brings to memory an amusing encounter. I was running for mayor of the City of New York in 1965. John Lindsay, the heavy favorite, was a friend and classmate of my brother James, who served as my campaign manager, and one day Lindsay communicated to him that he intended to give me a hard time on my alleged residence in New York (to run for mayor of New York you are required merely to have a residence there on the Election Day). Lindsay knew that I was an ardent citizen of Connecticut and a devotee of my home in Stamford.

He moved quickly. On a three-way television program the following day (with Abraham Beame, the Democratic candidate), he turned to me dramatically halfway through the program: "Bill, why don't you run for office in Connecticut, since that is where you live and intend to live?" "John," I said with arch seriousness "my ignorance of Connecticut politics is such that I do not even know the name of the mayor of Stamford." The following day Pope Paul came to New York. I was given two tickets by the Cardinal's office and filed into the cathedral with my son. Dressed in the garb of Knights of Malta, middle-aged men were acting as ushers. One of them approached me, smiled, led me to my pew, on reaching which he whispered in my ear, "Permit me to introduce myself,

Mr. Buckley. I am Walter Kennedy, the mayor of Stamford." I gave him a pious wink; and of course never worried that I might have hurt the feelings of the mayor of Stamford: Walter Kennedy knew all about the exigencies of politics.

During the long period in which urban renewal was fought out, an affluent neighbor told me that he worried greatly over any prospective new owner of *The Advocate,* the rumor having got out that Kingsley Gillespie, nearing 80, was looking for a potential buyer. Without saying so in as many words, he asked me whether I might approach Mr. Gillespie and just float out the idea that I was in contact with a potential purchaser.

Now Mr. Gillespie was not the most clubbable man in the history of Stamford and for that reason I was surprised, when I invited him to lunch, that he accepted; however, he specified that I should eat at his club — "that's where I always eat lunch," he explained, dispositively. I had previously said that in my company would be a gentleman who was seriously interested in the future of *The Advocate,* and so the three of us sat down, and I smiled breezily and asked whether it was true that *The Advocate* was for sale?

"Yes — to the right buyer, offering the right price."

"Oh, what is the right price?"

"I don't give it out."

"Aha. I can see your point, Well, what are your operating figures?"

"I don't give them out."

"Well, how is anybody supposed to know how much to offer you for *The Advocate*?"

"That's his problem."

After lunch I told my friend that if he wished to pursue his interest in acquiring *The Advocate,* he was on his own. We know only that the Times Mirror Co. materialized as the "right " person, offering the "right" price. Well, I am a columnist for the home paper and for that reason have to guard against sycophancy. But I can't help blurting it out: while it was a good paper under Mr. Gillespie, it is hard to dispute that it is a superb paper post-Gillespie, an object of civic pride.

For most people, the town they live in is a continuum of episodes, and I think now of three detachable ones which for me make up a theme.

Walter Wheeler called me on the telephone one day to tell me my contribution to the Stamford Hospital was "insufficient to take care of the hospital's needs." I was reminded that a few months before, during a cruise on his famous yawl, Cotton Blossom, a friend had dived into the water for a swim, suffered a heart attack, and died in the cockpit. As a token of remorseful self-abnegation, Walter Wheeler hauled out his boat for the rest of the season and let his friends know that he would donate the sum of money thus saved to the hospital, in memory of his dead friend. Walter Wheeler was a large character as well as a large man, the dynamic president of Pitney Bowes, an all-American competitor tracing back to his football days at Harvard. His enthusiasms were manifold, and included his business, the Democratic Party, racing his sloop to Bermuda, raising money for the Stamford Hospital —except for his collectivist politics, a character out of Ayn Rand. One man, only; but somehow, in the recent history of Stamford, I think of his long career as an episode.

A second reminiscence: late in the 1950's our weekend guests were the Villaverdes, daughter and son-in-law of Francisco Franco, the dictator of Spain. They wanted to see something of the residential parts of the area, and so, heading for the Merritt Parkway, I tooled down Summer Street toward Long Ridge Road. Just past the Sears Roebuck turn-off I came on a detour. I took the obligatory right turn, but instead of continuing on the indicated detour I thought to insinuate my way back on the principal road and quickly turned left.

We found ourselves like Dorothy in Oz — inside a community of perhaps twenty-five or thirty houses, each with about an acre or an acre and a half of land, each distinctive in its architecture, the trees billowing their greenness, the spring flowers clinging to every stave around the houses and garages, little streams running with cross-ways over them. The Villaverdes could not believe it. How much would such houses cost to buy? they asked. I said I didn't know, but they were weekending in a house for which I had paid

The spire of St. Mary's Roman Catholic Church dominates the skyline on Elm Street near Shippan Avenue.

$65,000 only eight years ago, and they could make their own projections.

This was a couple entirely at home in European castles, but it wasn't another castle they were wanting to look at; rather, they wanted to know what happens between a castle and the subordinate economic order, coming as they did from a country that skipped from the very rich to the very poor, with only a few morganatic burghers in between. They both rattled on excitedly that they had not seen such properties anywhere in Europe available to gentry of the middle class. I bowed my head with regal pride, and informed them that the United States is a land of opportunity, and that by current standards of poverty, 90 percent of us were poor at the turn of the century. I like to think that they took that thought back to Daddy, because the loosening of economic reins inside Spain, accompanied by the huge rise in personal income, was a major economic datum of the next 20 years.

And then the third episode, poignant, happy. It happens that I speak Spanish. This evolved into a familiarity with one or two Cubans when the flood of refugees from Castro began. At one point I teased my wife by telling her I thought of inserting a notice in *The Advocate* to announce "Buckley Cuban-American Refugee Hours, 3-5 Saturday afternoons." Now at one of these sessions, I was presented by a tearful young man with the plight of his brother who, together with his mother, hovered in Madrid awaiting a visa to the United States, which had been denied him on the grounds that his mother suffered from a disease. What, I asked solicitously, was the nature of this disease. "La senilidad." Senility. I laughed. Impossible, I reasoned, for United States immigration law or practice to deny entry to someone whose illness merely meant that he/she would die, that being what happens to everybody except bureaucrats. But the problem was real, because State Department regulations, fashioned around an agreement with Spain, specified that anyone taking refuge from Cuba in Spain bound for the United States who was in Spain for more than 90 days, would be returned to Cuba. So . . . I sent a telegram to our ambassador to Madrid, Robert Wagner, who during the mayoralty campaign I had once introduced to a friend as "my predecessor."

No answer.

The clock was ticking, and the poor mother and son had only 48 hours to go. So, I published a column aimed at the obtuseness of bureaucratic conduct; which resulted, one day after publication, in a telephone call from the deputy to the ambassador, advising me that the son had been contacted, he and his mother had visas, and they would arrive in New York the following day. There was the sweet sequel to the story. I invoked an old friendship with Fr. John Nagle of St. John's Church to intercede with me to permit the mother entry into a Catholic charities home. We went there together, and the Mother Superior was told that she must permit entry to the Cuban mother, never mind the long waiting list; after all, she had only days, maybe, to live. She lived, unconscious, in that charitable home, for seven years.

Meanwhile the young Cuban and his brother founded a grocery store in Stamford. It is open 12 hours a day for five days, and 16 hours a day on the sixth day. The brothers are not prosperous, but they are comfortable, their children are in school; and once again, the United States — specifically, Stamford — served as an asylum for those persecuted abroad.

I permitted myself to wonder, some time back, whether there was a great deal of that elusive substance — civic loyalty — in Stamford, whose population has been so transitory. But three or four years ago, Larry Gilgore, the talented conductor of the Stamford Chamber Orchestra, asked me to narrate Aaron Copland's "Lincoln Portrait" at Cummings Park on the Fourth of July, which of course I was glad to do. "There will be at least 10,000 people there," he said; and he was right. And they cheered the music and the patriotic festoonery and settled for me the question whether there is civic pride here, to the extent that it is a reflection of national pride. Stamford survives many dissatisfactions, among them the problems of finding living quarters. The nurse who attends my doctor told me that she is married to an architect who lives and works in Stamford and that in 10 years both of them, working as professionals, had not amassed enough money to buy a habitable condominium, let alone a house —so

Chamber musicians perform at St. Andrew's Episcopal Church on Washington Boulevard.

much for the dream of the late '50s witnessed by the Villaverdes. The recession has substantially altered these circumstances, but the relief recessions might bring in the way of cheaper real estate and business rentals is at the expense of somebody, and I think I detect a current of dissatisfaction, no doubt also a byproduct of the economic miasma that hit the state of Connecticut a few years ago when we went from being the most prosperous and best governed state in the union, to being one of the most heavily indebted and heavily taxed states in the union, with not very much relief in prospect.

Well, we are required to say as we reflect on the history of Stamford, it has always been so, has it not? The predatory Indians. The intramural civic strife. The Revolutionary War. The Industrial Revolution. The Civil War. The industrial losses after the First

World War, the gradual resuscitation during the 1930s, followed by the great expansion after the Second World War . . .

Stamford lives, and there are those, myself included, determined to live with it as long as life lasts. That inchoate harmony one feels with the house, the land, the civic center. It is ours, never mind that Greenwich is more beautiful, Norwalk more picturesque. We have a robust commercial and civic center with cultural landfills, we are an enclave in a large salt water sound stretching from the East River to Block Island Sound. And if ever we wonder how our predecessors in the area got themselves the reputation of Yankee Traders, we need only remind ourselves, with amusement, that in return for these 40 square miles, our ancestors paid out 12 coats, 12 hoes, 12 hatchets, 12 glasses, 12 knives, four kettles and four fathoms of white wampum. Mr. Gillespie, surveying the proposed exchange, would no doubt have said, solemnly and after meditation, that the price was right.

Before finishing my task, a brief explanation is required. Earlier I made a wisecrack about Stamford not being Athens. The remark traces back to an episode 25 years old. Monsignor John Hayes was the rector of St. Mary's Church, which was then mine (nowadays, on Sundays, I make the circuit of four or five churches). Monsignor was a highly educated man, especially engrossed in the work of Catholic authors in England during the twentieth century — Belloc, Chesterton, Waugh, Lunn. Sir Arnold Lunn had grown up in England and on leaving Oxford he cultivated simultaneously three professions. The first was mountaineering, the second, skiing, the third, philosophy. He was a formidable polemicist and in his 20s was determined to convert all the world to atheism, to which end he engaged Monsignor Ronald Knox, a famous Catholic convert, in a written debate published in book form. It was widely conceded that Lunn had outpointed even the learned Ronald Knox, but in one respect he failed. Because after giving long thought to his own contribution to the volume, and then to Knox's, Arnold Lunn went, a few months later, quietly to Oxford, where he asked Knox to baptize him in the Christian faith. He then wrote a book called, *Now I See,* which is still rated among the primary contributions to Christian apologetics.

My friendship with Lunn traced to my annual visits to Switzerland, where my wife and I came upon him. We skied together and became fast friends, and now he was coming to Stamford to stay the weekend. Monsignor Hayes heard about it and asked whether I might persuade the great man to give a lecture on Friday evening in the basement hall of St. Mary's. The plans made, at every mass for two Sundays running (that made, in total, about fourteen masses in those holy days) the laity were cajoled by Monsignor Hayes not to let the opportunity go by of attending the lecture on Friday by the great Arnold Lunn. Friday evening came, and the audience for him was about 50 people. After it was over we repaired to my house for food and drink. Ruminating over the small turnout, Monsignor Hayes sighed, "Well, Sir Arnold, Stamford is not exactly Athens."

It may not be Athens, dear reader, but it is the proud home to which we now proclaim: Happy Birthday!

Aerial of Stamford from Long Island Sound looking towards the northeast.

A Popular History of Stamford

with Illustrations

Don Russell and Mike Barlow

WHERE DO YOU BEGIN the history of a city? You can begin with a list of handy statistics, but that would leave a lot of questions unanswered.

For example, Stamford has 108,056 residents living in an area that covers just under 40 square miles.

But where did all those people come from?

There are 305 miles of paved streets in Stamford. At night those streets are lit by 11,091 street lights.

Who built those roads and put up those lights?

There are 82 churches and four synagogues in Stamford. Who worships at them?

Who attends the city's 11 public elementary schools, three middle schools and three high schools? Who attends the dozen or so private and parochial schools here?

Who plays in the city's 50 parks and recreational beaches?

Who stands ready at the city's 13 fire stations, two hospitals and one police station?

Who works in the 1,583 commercial buildings that stand in our city? Who labors in the 188 buildings that are classified industrial?

Who lives in the city's 21,609 homes? And who lives in the 9,183 condos?

Who drives the 80,354 automobiles registered in Stamford?

The figures are interesting, but they don't really begin to tell the story of our city.

To understand Stamford, you must go back to the beginning, before there were roads, shopping malls, office buildings, condos or even houses.

To understand Stamford, you must begin in a place that is not Stamford. Because the history of Stamford began in a town that many of us have seen only on a map.

THE POPULATION OF STAMFORD had grown to 2,700 by the time of the French and Indian War. That grisly conflict, known in Europe as the Seven Years War, permanently established Anglo-Saxon as the dominant culture of the North American continent. But the victory had unexpected consequences. One was the realization by the colonists that they could fight and win a large-scale war against a formidable enemy. They had tasted blood and were proud of the part they had played in helping Britain achieve success.

Then there was the sticky question of who would actually pick up the check. Britain figured the colonies should pay for the war because it was fought to protect their security. The colonists thought otherwise. From their perspective, it was just another chapter in the centuries-old power struggle between the British and the French. Let them pay for it.

Seen from this viewpoint, it's easy to understand why the colonists were enraged when Britain unilaterally decided that the best way to settle its war debt was to raise taxes in America. Anger over these taxes rippled through the colonies. British policy became the subject of public protest. In Stamford, Webb's Tavern was the site of a "tea execution" in June 1775. Flanked by armed soldiers, a shipment of tea was paraded through town before being strung up on a gibbet in front of the popular tavern, which stood on what is now the corner of Bank and Main streets. The tea, judged "guilty" of being heavily taxed by the British Parliament, was then burned to the delight of the large crowd that had gathered.

By the same time next year, the situation had become less humorous. Like many other communities, Stamford was split into two camps: rebels who favored independence and Tories who favored continued loyalty to the Crown. Tory families were often forced from their homes by rebel sympathizers. Pro-rebellion leaders were often the targets of Tory attacks. One outspoken clergyman, the Rev. Moses Mather, along with four of his sons, was kidnapped from his parsonage in August of 1779 and taken to the British stronghold in New York. He was eventually released and returned to Stamford, where he continued to speak out against the Crown. So the Tories kidnapped him again, this time in broad

Mural shows the Post Road stagecoach stopping at Webb's Tavern. George Washington ate breakfast at this venerable inn which stood at One Bank Street.

daylight in front of his entire congregation. The rebellious minister and many of his parishioners were tied up and taken by boat to Long Island, where they spent several months in prison.

Mather's church was in a section of Stamford called Middlesex. The area is now a part of Darien, but the old church is still there, on Brookside Road.

As the rebellion spread, many Stamford Tories decided that migrating to Long Island was the better part of valor, at least until the hostilities ceased. Not content to merely sit out the war, however, they plagued Stamford from across the Sound with raids launched from Lloyd's Neck. Finally, on the night of Sept. 5, 1779, the rebels managed to launch a counterstrike. Major Benjamin Tallmadge led a force of 130 hand-picked men from Shippan Point to Lloyd's Neck, where the surprised Tories quickly surrendered.

A plaque at the Stamford Yacht Club now marks the area from which Tallmadge's force took off.

Tallmadge, who served as General George Washington's chief of intelligence, played a critical role in the unraveling of Benedict Arnold's plot to turn West Point over to the British. On Sept. 23, 1780, a man who called himself John Anderson was captured near Tarrytown. Tallmadge happened to arrive on the scene in time to prevent the prisoner from being sent forward to Arnold. It was a fortuitous moment in history, because Anderson was in fact a British major named John André. In his boot were found papers incriminating Arnold, who was still a popular and trusted general. To the regret of Tallmadge, Major André, who was merely doing his duty as a British officer, was hanged. Arnold, a Norwich native who had been considered a brilliant commander, managed to escape to Canada. In 1781 he led a British raid on New London, cementing his image as the American Brutus. He later fled to England, where he lived the rest of his days, branded as a traitor by both sides.

Col. Benjamin Tallmadge from a pencil sketch by Col. John Trumbull.

Fort Stamford as it appears today.

The grave of Gen. David Waterbury in Woodland Cemetery.

That Stamford was spared a major attack was partly due to the construction of Fort Stamford, commanded by General David Waterbury. The fort was Waterbury's brainchild and he managed to convince his friend, George Washington, that it was essential to the defense of the region. From the fortress, defenders had a clear view of the Sound, preventing the British from mounting a sneak attack. The fort's remaining earthworks, as well as a more recently erected monument, are off Westover Road in Stamford's Roxbury section. The area is heavily wooded now, but back in the colonial era it had been cleared for farming. Waterbury's grave can be seen at Woodland Cemetery in the city's South End.

BY 1800, STAMFORD'S POPULATION had grown to 4,465. There were now six churches — four Congregational, one Episcopal and one Baptist. Religion still exerted a mighty influence on the town. Squads of roving deacons would monitor the highways to make sure no one broke the Sabbath rules.

Down at Lockwood's Landing, ships bound for New York or Long Island would stock up on Connecticut potatoes, apples, corn, wool or livestock. Stagecoaches rattling between New York and New Haven would stop at Leed's Tavern on Main Street, since Stamford was seen as a convenient midpoint on the dusty trip along the Post Road. And General Lafayette paid a visit to Stamford in 1824, stopping at the home of Major John Davenport. The Davenport house sat at the present corner of Summer and Main. A popular restaurant stands there now.

In 1829, *The Intelligencer*, precursor to *The Advocate*, was started. One of the newspaper's first big stories was the establishment of downtown Stamford as a separate borough in 1830.

The borough covered an area about three-quarters of a mile square. Within its boundaries were 68 dwellings, 5 churches, 11 stores, 28 mechanic shops, two public and five private schools, a

Stage Street as it appeared in the early 1900s. Stagecoach drivers would stop there to exchange their tired horses for fresh ones. The site is now the Town Center garage.

The Hon. John Davenport.

Stagecoach days were recreated on Main Street by the Vanderbilt family in the early 1900s.

Two young sailors pose for a tintype in the mid-19th century.

Knapp's Dock, the depot at the head of the Mill River inlet in the South End.

printing office, a flour mill, a large tannery and three stone buildings for rolling iron, according to the newspaper.

The borough's 633 inhabitants were governed by the Board of Burgesses, chaired by a warden, who served as the borough's chief executive. The Board of Burgesses was the venerable ancestor of our present 40-member Board of Representatives. The old panel, however, had only seven members to oversee the emerging nucleus of today's city.

It's hard to imagine now, but back in those days Stamford residents would drive their cattle down Long Ridge and High Ridge Roads, stopping to spend the night at Bull's Head before continuing on down Bedford Street to load their herds aboard ships for transport to markets up and down the Atlantic seaboard.

There was even a fair amount of direct trade between Stamford and the West Indies. Sloops would sail into the harbor's East Branch, then maneuver up a canal to unload their cargoes in the middle of town. The canal has since been filled in and covered over, but the street bearing its name still runs to the harbor.

WHEN STAMFORD CELEBRATED its bicentennial in 1841, it still considered itself a typical Yankee community, complete with an annual meeting on the first Monday of every October. Ethnically and spiritually, Stamford residents were a virtually homogenous group — white Anglo-Saxon Protestants. This situation would soon change.

In December 1848, the first locomotive puffed into town. It was a momentous event in more ways than one. For several years prior to the railroad's arrival, the population of Stamford had actually been in decline, mostly due to the separation of Darien and New Canaan from the town. The community, which had grown accustomed to steady growth, entered an anxious period of economic stagnation as business and trade fell off.

The clanking iron horse rescued the town from its downward spiral. Stamford was now a link on the chain between New York and New Haven. As the economic picture brightened, Stamford became a magnet for hundreds, and then thousands, of job-hungry immigrants. The railroad also brought commuters from New York.

These newcomers, along with those who followed, infused puritanical Stamford with new vitality. Suddenly there were tailors, bakers, sculptors, painters, singers and poets. As the community became more of a melting pot, the grim Yankee stoicism that had characterized early life here faded. It was replaced by a new energy, one that fueled itself on diversity, rather than uniformity.

DEPOT OF THE N. Y. & N. H. R. R., AT STAMFORD, 1867.

Built in the fashionable Second Empire style, this railroad depot stood several hundred feet north of the site of the present station.

The Rowland mural shows the first locomotive train arriving in Stamford on Christmas Day, 1848. By the next year, three daily commuter trains ran between New Haven and New York.

THE MATTER OF WHETHER TO SOLVE the slavery issue with cannon or compromise was settled on April 12, 1861, the day Confederate artillery shelled the Union garrison at Fort Sumter, S.C. If opinion in Stamford was divided before the rebel attack on the fort, news of the Union surrender there two days later galvanized support for swift retaliation. When President Abraham Lincoln called for volunteers, the citizens of Stamford responded promptly.

Before the hostilities, Connecticut Gov. William Buckingham had foreseen the need to strengthen the state militia. Stamford had pitched in by forming the Stamford Light Guards, under the command of Captain Lorenzo Meeker. When Lincoln issued the call to arms, Stamford held a public meeting to respond.

John Davenport, whose grandfather and great-grandfather had fought in the Revolution, was on hand for the meeting, along with former Gov. William T. Minor, Thomas G. Ritch , H.F. Osborn, the Rev. P.S. Evans, the Rev. E.B. Huntington, Jacob Krieg, G.B. Glendinning and James Betts. According to reports at the time, these leading citizens addressed the meeting with "one voice," advocating a vigorous prosecution of the war.

In fact, 30 of Stamford's young men had already affixed their names to a list of volunteers led by Theodore Miller and Theodore Delacroix. A committee consisting of businessmen James H. Hoyt,

Capt. Isaac Hoyt of Stamford died of the 'local fever' in the Civil War.

Capt. Charles A. Hobby of Company B, one of six Stamford brothers who fought in the Civil War.

Isaac Quintard, Charles Brown, William Skiddy and Albert Seeley was appointed to raise funds. A sum of $4,500 was hurriedly pledged to the cause. And as a symbol of their resolve to save the Union, Stamford residents agreed to erect a flagpole 150 feet high in what is now known as Veterans Park. The flagpole served Stamford during the war and for the next 25 years.

Following the departure of the first company of volunteers, Stamford citizens formed the Soldiers Aid Society. It helped supply comfort to the soldiers in the field and aid for sick and wounded veterans recuperating in hospitals. One such infirmary was on David's Island, off the coast of New Rochelle.

A fair for the society was held in Seeley's Hall in the summer of 1861. Stamford women were credited with the success of the fair, which raised $3,500 in cash. Two weeks later the people of Stamford contributed another $2,500 to the people of East Tennessee. Stamford residents had been touched by the plight of these Southerners who had been impoverished by their refusal to join the cause of the South.

Stamford was also a stop on the Underground Railroad, the secret network designed to speed runaway slaves to sanctuary in the North. Benjamin Daskam was the "station master."

The people of Stamford rallied above and beyond the call of duty in practically every area of wartime activity. By volunteering to fight, by keeping the home fires burning and by helping other less fortunate towns and states, Stamford played its part in the epic war to reunite the nation.

More than 500 Stamford residents served in the Union army. Of that number, 122 died. The names of all who served, along with the names of Stamford residents who fought in the French and Indian War, the American Revolution, the War of 1812, the Mexican War, the Spanish American War and World War I, are inscribed on a stone monument in St. John's Park at the intersection of Tresser Boulevard and Main Street.

Seeley's Hall on East Main Street in 1935.

IN 1868, HENRY R. TOWNE AND LINUS YALE JR. decided that Stamford, with its ready access to rail and water, would be the ideal place to manufacture their innovative pin-tumbler locks. Yale died unexpectedly of a heart attack on Christmas, but Towne went ahead with their plans to build a shop in Hoytville, a section of Stamford that lay between the ship canal and the railroad tracks. In May of the following year, the Yale Lock Co. opened its doors. By the 1890s, one out of every 16 Stamford residents would be employed by the firm. One of the nation's great entrepreneurs, Towne served as president of the company until 1915.

The tremendous success of this venture ignited an era of rapid growth that completed Stamford's transformation from a rural community with some manufacturing to an industrial center with some farms.

Other major manufacturing concerns followed in Yale's footsteps and found motivated workers and high profits in Stamford. Their early ranks included companies such as Schleicher, the piano manufacturer whose plant was on Pacific Street. Nearby was the Collender Billiard Co., which made billiard tables and balls. It later burned down in a spectacular blaze fed by the cans of varnish

The Yale Lock Company shortly after it opened in 1869.

The former Yale & Towne complex as it looks today. More than half of the thirty buildings that stood on the South End site were demolished in the early 1980s.

ABOVE: *The bank lock room of the Yale & Towne factory in 1892.* ■ BELOW: *Henry R. Towne lived two blocks from the factory complex in 'Rockland,' an elegant Queen Anne-style house on Atlantic Street.*

ABOVE: *Judge John Clasen, founder of Stamford Hospital, with his team of oxen.* ■ BELOW: *The old Scofield residence on Soundview Avenue as it looks today.*

and sealant used to make the tables. Phillips Chemical, known for its laxatives, had a large facility in Glenbrook. Another major enterprise, the Stamford Manufacturing Co., was in the Cove section. It handled imports of licorice and dye.

The Blickensderfer factory was located just below the railroad bridge on Atlantic Avenue. Like Yale & Towne (the company formally changed its name in 1883), Blickensderfer also pioneered a modern product we now take for granted: the portable typewriter. George C. Blickensderfer, who lived on Bedford Street across from the First Congregational Church, was issued his patent in 1892.

As industry moved in, Stamford developed into a modern, prosperous community. The fire department was reorganized to include full-time professionals as well as volunteers. The Stamford Water Co. was established to ensure a reliable supply of safe drinking water. The Stamford Gas Light Co. was formed to provide power for businesses and homes. By 1890, the population of Stamford was 15,700.

The Schleicher Piano Factory on South Pacific Street.
The building is now the home of Pacific Plumbing &
Heating Supply Co.

The Collender Billiard Table factory on South Pacific Street.

STANDARD AMERICAN BILLIARD TABLES

New Design, Patented June 6, 1871, and December 23, 1873.

An advertisement for the tables.

Entered according to Act of Congress, by H. W. COLLENDER, in Office of Librarian of Congress, Washington, 1871
The above design is made in Walnut, Rosewood, Hungarian Ash, or other woods.
The STANDARD AMERICAN TABLES are furnished with the unrivalled PHELAN & COLLENDER COMBINA-
TION CUSHION, demanded by all intelligent amateur players, and used by experts in all their important test games.

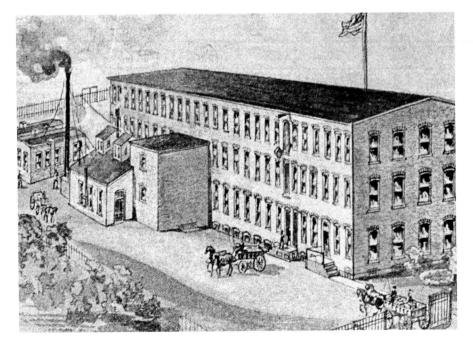

The Blickensderfer Typewriter Company on Atlantic Street. The building later was the home of Schick Dry Shavers.

'The Terrace,' home of inventor George C. Blickensderfer on Bedford Street.

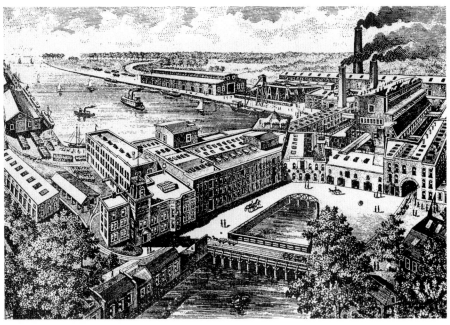

The Stamford Manufacturing Company at Cove Island.

The Stamford Water Company's waterfall off Lakeside Drive.

STAMFORD MARKED ITS 250th BIRTHDAY with a celebration that drew more than 30,000 visitors. But, despite the festivities, it was apparent that the community's growth had rendered its antique forms of government obsolete. Government officials were mostly unpaid volunteers who tended to come from Stamford's wealthier quarters. Although the densely populated borough existed within the boundaries of the sparsely populated town, each had its own government. It was an awkward situation, to say the least.

On Sept. 9, 1892, the Board of Burgesses convened a citizen assembly to discuss the creation of the City of Stamford. Three days later a charter committee was formed. It was made up of leading citizens such as Oliver Fessenden, a wholesale jeweler; W.D. Smith, a coal dealer and banker; William W. Skiddy, president of the Stamford Manufacturing Co.; Charles Lounsbury, a shoe manufacturer who traced his lineage back to the original settlers; Charles Getman, a lumber dealer; Schuyler Merritt, an executive at Yale & Towne; and Dr. Henry Gieb, a bank director.

In November, the committee went public with its report. To the surprise and consternation of the committee, the plan aroused a storm of protest. The residents of Glenbrook did not want to be included in the new city. There was strong criticism of the committee's plan to divide the city into four wards. And the elite composition of the small committee itself raised suspicions.

Stamford celebrates its 250th birthday.

Postcard of the old YMCA on Atlantic Street

This postcard shows the present-day Post Office.

Postcard of the Congregational Church on Bedford Street.

ABOVE: *Main Street looking east in 1905. The old Stamford Savings Bank is on the right.* ■ BELOW: *The Rowland mural depicts Atlantic Street with Town Hall in the background.*

Other milestones of the early 1900s included the construction of the YMCA and the Post Office buildings on Atlantic Street. The Stamford Theater was opened on the site of the present Stamford Center for the Arts. The Congregational Church that had long stood on the corner of Bank and Atlantic was moved to the head of Bedford Park, now Latham Park. The granite blocks used to build the church were cut from a quarry off Grove Street.

By now, Stamford's population was increasing at an average rate of about 1,000 persons a year and government was obliged to consider a host of problems typical to growing cities. Street paving and maintenance, sidewalk widening, police and fire protection, traffic control, sanitation, health, education — all the modern services we take more or less for granted today were being tackled on a large scale for the first time.

Historian Herbert Sherwood captures the headstrong spirit of this era in his book, *The Story of Stamford.* He describes early 20th century Stamford as a place that was " . . . hustle and bustle . . . the smooth street pavements are crowded with traffic. As far as the eye can reach in every direction the streets are bordered with business blocks and parked automobiles . . . It is a new city."

Three Stamford leaders, circa 1913. From left, Mayor Walter Austin, Fire Chief Harry Parker and Police Chief William Brennan.

AS WE APPROACH the end of the millennium with a queasy mixture of dread and relief, it's startling to recall the exuberance and optimism with which Western Civilization greeted the 20th century. It was generally assumed that our rapidly burgeoning technologies would solve the world's problems and that the century that lay ahead would be one characterized by peace, fulfillment and harmony.

Little did we know that the status quo in Europe was about to be shattered forever and that America would be drawn into the ensuing conflict.

Battery F parades down Main Street during World War I.

Into the maelstrom that was World War I rushed the naively heroic Americans. We would emerge as a different people — older and wiser, with a new set of worldly responsibilities.

Like every other community in the nation, Stamford carried its share of the burden. Twenty-four hundred Stamford residents served in the Army and Navy during WW I, also called the Great War and the War to End All Wars. Thirty-eight Stamford residents died in the service of their country — 18 of disease, 14 in combat, three by drowning, two in airplane accidents and one in an automobile accident.

A special booklet issued in 1919 to commemorate the return of the surviving Stamford veterans recounts how some of their less fortunate comrades met their fates. There was Augusto Fornaciari, brother of Joseph Fornaciari of 177 West Main Street. He was killed in action in France on Sept. 18, 1918, while serving with Company G, 39th Infantry, Fourth Division. He was 23 years old and had worked for the New Haven Railroad.

And there was Frank T. Rivers, son of Mrs. Tolman Rivers of Long Ridge, who died after being shot in the abdomen near the Bois d'Etraves in France. He had worked at Faucett Haberdashery before the war.

Samuel Tresser, son of Mr. and Mrs. Morris Tresser, of 83 Hawthorn Street, was killed in action on Aug. 24, 1918, outside a town called Fismes in France. It was an unlucky place for Stamford residents. A few nights before, Oscar H. Cowan, son of Mr. and Mrs. James Cowan of North Stamford, had been killed there by an exploding shell. He was buried in the churchyard in the nearby village of Mareuil-en-Dole.

George Fortunis, of 116 Broad St., had been an employee of the Olympia Candy Co. Killed in action shortly before the signing of the Armistice, he had been one of Stamford's first draftees.

Charles Drake Mills, son of Mr. and Mrs. Francis D. Mills, of 54 River Street, was lost when his ship, the Navy tug Gyspy Queen, struck a rock and sank near Arme Light off the coast of France on April 28, 1919. His body was not recovered.

David Wagner, son of Mr. and Mrs. Samuel Wagner, died when the transport Tuscania was sunk by a German submarine off the coast of Scotland. A lifetime Stamford resident, Wagner had been on his way to France with the 20th Engineers. He was buried at Port Ellen on the Isle of Islay.

AT LEFT: *John C. Latham, winner of a Congressional Medal of Honor in World War I. Bedford Park was renamed for him in 1970.* AT RIGHT: *WWI memorial now in Veterans Park.*

Arthur Pitney

Walter Bowes

Stamford industry also did its part to further the war effort. In Waterside, the Luders Marine Construction Co. made submarine chasers, speedy vessels that the Allies hoped would help even the odds in the North Atlantic. Luders also was contracted to manufacture tugs, barges and motor launches for the military.

By 1918, Stamford residents were hard at work in a variety of shops making hand grenades, fuses, airplane parts, firing pins and other needed items. There was even a plant in town that manufactured tear gas.

Amid the tumult of war and its aftermath, few took note of an event that occurred in 1919. In was in that year that Walter Bowes merged his Stamford-based stamping company with Arthur Pitney's Chicago-based postage meter company to form Pitney Bowes. For decades the company has been one of the city's largest employers and a major source of tax revenue.

ON DEC. 24, 1928, President Calvin Coolidge gave a valedictory address to Congress. "Never before have times been better, with wages high, business good, taxes reduced, and the national debt one-third paid off," Coolidge told the lawmakers. "America is at peace with the world; notable steps have been taken to outlaw war; weak and struggling nations have been helped along the road to sovereignty and stability."

History proved his optimism to be unfounded. Within a year, the stock market had crashed. The prosperity of the Roaring '20s vanished as the nation slipped into the grim depths of the Great Depression.

By 1932, banks across the land were failing and factories were closing. The sight of unemployed businessmen selling apples on streetcorners became commonplace. Families lost their homes. The lucky ones went to live with relatives. The less fortunate sought shelter in churches or lived outdoors.

Although Stamford was not spared, some of the pain was eased by careful planning and an uncommon spirit of cooperation. Perhaps this spirit was a holdover from the community's early days, when hardship was considered a test of Yankee character.

There are many examples of how Stamford residents pulled together to survive those dark days. They set up soup kitchens and

Whitman Bailey drawing of Columbus Park in 1928.

planted vegetable gardens. They provided shelter for the poor and indigent. They forgave loans and extended credit to families strapped for cash.

Richard Henry Gillespie Jr., general manager of *The Advocate*, personally spoke to advertisers who had fallen behind on their payments. Gillespie told them that *The Advocate* wanted to keep their business and did not expect full payment until the economy had turned around. In the meantime, he said, they could pay whatever amount they could reasonably afford. Gillespie's tactic assured a steady flow of cash, even through the leanest years.

Local banks adopted similar practices, realizing that patience and flexibility — not qualities normally associated with bankers back then — would allow them to survive. These policies ultimately paid off. Throughout all the years of the Depression, only one Stamford bank failed.

Government reacted, predictably, by laying off some employees and cutting the salaries of others. The school budget was slashed and the annual Fourth of July fireworks celebration was cancelled. The post office graciously announced that it would give preference to married men when hiring extra help for the Christmas rush.

Handbill protests beatings of May Day marchers.

BUT THE DEPRESSION wasn't all bad news. In 1933, President Roosevelt began putting together the New Deal, a series of national policies and new laws aimed at restoring confidence in the economy. Banks were reopened, bankrupt farmers were given the chance to repurchase their farms and vast sums were allocated for a wide variety of public works projects across the nation.

In 1934, Fairfield County began work on its own spectacular project — The Merritt Parkway. More than 2,000 people were employed in the construction of the road, which runs through 38 miles of verdant Connecticut countryside. Since the parkway's completion in 1940, some of the beautiful Art Deco designs carved into its stone bridges have become nationally famous.

In Stamford, construction of a new high school sports stadium began under the aegis of the federal Works Progress Administration. Boyle Stadium, as it's now known, was one of several federally financed projects undertaken in Stamford during the Depression. Other WPA projects here included bridges, roads and dams.

The Merritt Parkway, looking west, near Long Ridge Road.

One of a pair of WPA-sponsored statues by Henry Kreis at Fairfield Court Apartments, Stamford's first public housing complex.

Girls field hockey game at Boyle Stadium behind Stamford High School.

Local business groups played their part in the recovery, too, banding together to promote their neighborhoods. Merchants organized on Bedford Street, Davenport Square, Main Street, West Park Street and River Street. Summer Street was widened to accommodate more stores and traffic.

And even though Yale & Towne moved some of its departments out of town, the loss was offset by the arrival of the Petroleum Heat and Power Co., which transferred its Chicago operations to Stamford.

By the late 1930s, the darkness had begun to lift. Soon Stamford would be involved in its next major challenge — preparing for another world war.

BY 1941, STAMFORD BOASTED 42 churches, 20 public schools and two parochial schools. Stamford Hospital had 270 beds. A second hospital, St. Joseph Medical Center, was on the drawing boards. The Ferguson Library now had 95,000 volumes. There were five golf courses, six hotels and five movie theaters — the largest seating 2,500 patrons.

Local industries were thriving again, producing such diverse items as roller bearings, trunk locks, loud speakers, brass oil burners, x-ray tubes, electric motors, rolled metals, electric shavers, stoves, furniture, lift trucks, toys and sheet metal.

Beautiful homes, many built in the gracious styles of the previous century, adorned the hills and lined the shore. There was an abundant supply of pure water, piped from lakes eight miles north of the city.

Thanks to the war in Europe, Stamford was back on its feet. Swing was king. Radio provided hours of daily entertainment, with shows like "Jack Benny," "Gangbusters," "Fibber McGee and Molly," and "The Shadow."

Atlantic Street in the early 1940s. The area between the bank and the Sears building is now occupied by a traffic ramp to the Town Center parking garage.

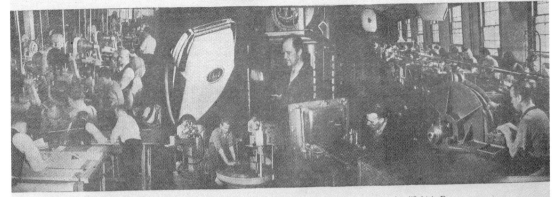

Advertisements show wide range of products manufactured in Stamford.

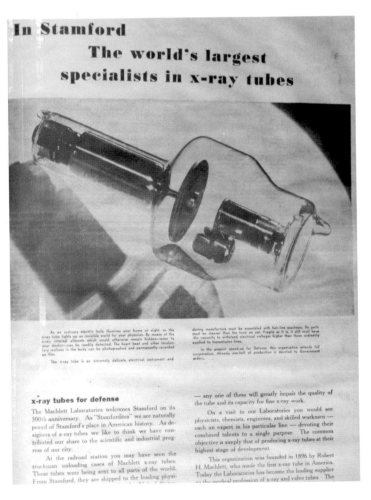

Mayor Alfred Phillips campaigned against American involvement in yet another world war. After Pearl Harbor, however, Stamford backed the war effort solidly. Stamford's contributions ranged from Victory Gardens to PT boats.

Although the headlines told of Nazi conquests in Europe, the war still seemed remote — until Dec. 7, 1941. With the infamous sneak attack by Japan on Pearl Harbor, the illusion of security was shattered. The bold headline in the next day's edition of *The Advocate* read: "Congress Declares War." Another Page 1 story that day told of how 20 Stamford residents immediately volunteered to fight. Yet another story detailed how Stamford had "swung into action today to put this community of sixty-one thousand inhabitants on a strict wartime footing. Police guards were doubled at factory, water supply, power and other vital stations, civilian groups were lining up for the protection of house and home, and the order was out to round up Japanese nationals. No time was lost by official and volunteer defense forces . . ."

The community gardens started during the Depression were renamed Victory Gardens to help the war effort. Everyone was

Mayor Charles Moore, left, encourages contributions for war relief.

urged to buy war bonds. Essential products, such as meat, leather and gasoline, were rationed. Local industries switched over to military production. Luders Marine manufactured PT boats. Yale & Towne made parts for tanks. Pitney Bowes proved it could make periscopes for submarines.

In all, more than 10,000 Stamford residents — men and women — served in the armed forces during World War II. One hundred ninety-five of them lost their lives in the fight for democracy.

The post-war era was a time of giddy expansion, as returning veterans used their GI loans to buy houses and start families. In 1949, Stamford's town and city governments were finally united. A Board of Representatives was created to be the city's new legislative council.

The 1950 census put Stamford's population at 74,293. The following year, a study by the planning board concluded that Stamford's theoretical population center had moved north during the last 10 years and was now located on a vacant parcel of land owned by the city near the intersection of Hoyt and Bedford streets. The Board of Representatives recommended that the land, which had been used for growing vegetables during the war, be set aside for the construction of a new police and court building. Planning Director Walter Wachter attributed the northward movement of the city's population center to the rapid growth of Springdale and Glenbrook.

Other front-page items that year included a tiff between Mayor Thomas F.J. Quigley and the Board of Representatives over the cost of furnishing the mayor's office in Town Hall. Quigley asked for $3,500. The board reduced the amount to $2,000. When a reporter asked the mayor how he intended to spend the money, the mayor snapped, "None of your business!"

The Advocate carried wire service stories about fighting in Korea and it was not uncommon to see stories about city residents in uniform who were wounded in action. Also in the news at this time were attempts to crack down on speeding on the Merritt Parkway, where commuter traffic was becoming a daily problem.

I F YOU LOOKED AT AN aerial photo of downtown Stamford taken 30 years ago, you would not see the city we know today.

To be quite frank, it was not a pretty sight back then. Clusters of ugly tenements surrounded the railroad yards between Jefferson and State Streets. Main Street was U.S. Route 1 and it ran uninterrupted through the center of town. There was no Tresser Boulevard, only Meadow Street, a busy path crowded with small shops and private homes. Washington Boulevard was Washington Avenue, a two-lane strip that stretched from Broad to Woodside.

Stamford's industrial base, once the source of pride and jobs, had withered as companies relocated to the South and West —regions of the country where labor costs tended to be cheaper.

By the late 1950s, the city's core had decayed badly. Although many residents acknowledged the need for action to arrest the city's downward slide, they were unable to agree on a proper course of action.

The city's inability to reach a consensus on urban renewal was particularly vexing because the federal government was offering major financing for approved projects. But critics of urban renewal

Rooftop view of part of downtown Stamford scheduled for demolition during urban renewal in the 1970s. More than 1,000 families and 400 businesses were relocated.

View of East Main Street in the 1960s, before urban renewal.

pointed to the fiasco in New Haven, where large parcels of land had been cleared and left vacant.

In the early 1960s, Mayor J. Walter Kennedy lobbied the Board of Finance to earmark $1 million for urban renewal. The money was needed to convince Washington that Stamford was serious about fixing up its downtown. Kennedy was an ardent supporter of urban renewal, but he wasn't able to convince the board to go along. When Kennedy resigned to become president of the National Basketball Association, Judge William Hickey was appointed to finish out his term. It wasn't until the election of Mayor Thomas Mayers in 1963 that the city approved the funds.

Mayers, a Bloomingdale's executive, presented his plan to the Board of Finance in person — a bold tactic that went back to the days of Homer Cummings. When the board members wavered, Mayers persuaded them to do the right thing, arguing that the money was not a giveaway but an investment in the city's future. Approval from the Board of Representatives soon followed and, as the former mayor recently recalled, "We were off and running!"

ABOVE: *The Yale & Towne strike of 1945-46 caused considerable bitterness. By 1959, Yale & Towne closed its Stamford operation completely.* ■ BELOW: *Part of Pacific Street in the 1960s before urban renewal.*

Groundbreaking for GTE in 1973. Mayor Julius Wilensky is driving the bulldozer. Developer Robert N. Rich, left, looks over plans with Leslie Warner of GTE and Urban Redevelopment Commission Chairman James Carey.

The project remained on the city agenda during the administration of the next mayor, Bruno Giordano. And when his successor, Julius Wilensky, was elected, urban renewal took another giant leap forward. Wilensky was able to settle many of the lawsuits that arose from the project, which involved clearing vast tracts of private land for redevelopment.

Interest in the project continued during the administration of Mayor Frederick Lenz. But the next mayor, Louis Clapes, is credited with shepherding the effort through some of its most difficult stages.

Mayers recalled how he and former Mayor Wilensky took Clapes to lunch after his election. "We told him, 'You're the guy that can get this done,' and by golly, he did!"

Determined not to follow the example set by New Haven, which had knocked down a huge chunk of its downtown without having a specific developer waiting in the wings to rebuild it,

St. John's Towers, a low and moderate income apartment complex, was completed in 1971. The three buildings provide more than 350 housing units.

Landmark Tower, the 21-story signature building for the new downtown, was completed in the early 1970s.

ABOVE: *Historic buildings on Atlantic Street as seen through Veterans Park.* ■ BELOW: *The statue of Christopher Columbus presides over the park named for him. Here, local farmers sell their produce during summer months.*

PREVIOUS PAGES: *First double-page spread shows Tresser Boulevard at dusk. At left foreground is the headquarters of General Re Corporation. Second spread shows a school bus on Erskine Road in North Stamford. The third captures a beautiful sunrise over Peck Point.*

ABOVE: *Picturesque totem polls welcome visitors to the Stamford Museum and Nature Center off High Ridge Road.* ■ BELOW: *At the Nature Center, former estate of Henri Bendel, pitching pennies and listening to the falling water help pass a hot summer day.*

Visitors feed the ducks and geese at the Museum and Nature Center.

ABOVE: *A youth baseball game in Scalzi Park is one of many activities the park offers year-round.*
BELOW: *Public tennis courts at Scalzi Park attract participants of all ages.*

Basketball at Scalzi Park ranges from organized recreational leagues to pickup games such as this.

An inverted ziggurat, the GTE building on Tresser Boulevard was designed by Stamford architect, Victor Bisharat.

ABOVE: *Canterbury Green, a mixture of offices, shops and apartments, rises over the late 19th century Gothic St. John's Episcopal Church.* ■ BELOW: *St. Andrew's Episcopal Church on Washington Boulevard retains the Victorian Gothic rectory designed by H. Hudson Holly.*

St. John's Towers on Washington Boulevard, as seen from its plaza-level playground.

ABOVE: *Sailboats skim along Long Island Sound during the annual Mayor's Cup Race.*
BELOW: *Runners race along Long Ridge Road during the 1990 Stamford Classic Marathon.*

ABOVE: *Stamford High School takes on Stamford Catholic High School in their annual football game.*
BELOW: *Sledders enjoy the winter snow at E. Gaynor Brennan Golf Course.*

ABOVE: *Some of "Stamford's finest" in front of the police station on Bedford Street.* ▪ BELOW: *Firefighters at the Main Street firehouse, across from Canterbury Green.*

ABOVE: *A Board of Representatives committee meets at the Stamford Government Center.* ■ BELOW: *An English as Second Language class helps smooth a newcomer's transition into the mainstream of American life.*

ABOVE: *The 150-year-old Galen Carter House is now the rectory of St. John's Roman Catholic Church.*
BELOW: *The garden on the plaza of St. John's Towers is well-tended.*

Metro Center is an architecturally-acclaimed office building across from the Transportation Center.

The Pink Tent Festival of the Arts has been a late June fixture in Mill River Park for more than a decade.

ABOVE: *The German-American Club in Glenbrook retains its tradition of lively song and dance.*
BELOW: *The Festival of Saint Theodore provides a religious and cultural focus for Stamford's Italian community.*

ABOVE: *Another popular attraction is the annual fair held on the grounds of the Greek Orthodox Church of the Annunciation on Newfield Avenue.* ■ BELOW: *Old-time traditions are upheld at The Hibernian Club by gaily-dressed practitioners of the jig and reel.*

ABOVE: *The modern Agudath Sholom Synagogue on Strawberry Hill Avenue upholds the traditions of Orthodox Judaism.* ■ BELOW: *The Long Ridge Congregational Church, a Greek Revival-style church dates back to the late 1800s, when Long Ridge was a rural settlement.*

The First Presbyterian Church on Bedford Street is more commonly known as the "Fish Church" because of its shape.

business to Edgar Hoyt. Whether Hoyt's timing was a matter of luck or foresight is unknown. What we do know, however, is that the railroad came to Stamford in December of that same year. Its arrival would transform the uniformly Yankee community into a bustling melting pot, a vital link in a chain of burgeoning communities up and down the coast.

Hoyt followed Holly's tradition of emphasizing local news. As Stamford grew and became more sophisticated, so did the local newspaper. In 1860, Hoyt sold the business to William Speers Campbell. Campbell stayed with *The Stamford Advocate,* as it was now known, until his death in 1867.

It was during Campbell's tenure that the Gillespie family initially became associated with the newspaper. They would be linked with *The Stamford Advocate* for the next 117 years.

William Wright Gillespie moved to Stamford from Canada in 1861. He was 21 years old and a journeyman printer. He managed to talk his brother, Edward Thomas Wright Gillespie, into joining him at *The Stamford Advocate.* E.T.W., as he was called, covered the Civil War for the paper, filing dispatches from the front that still make for compelling reading. "A trainload of wounded and dying men presented a sad spectacle, the motion of the cars had aggravated the pain of their wounds, and the air was filled with their cries and groans," he wrote in 1862.

By 1866, William Gillespie had formed a partnership with Campbell. When Campbell died the following year, the Gillespies assumed control. In 1883, the business was turned over to E.T.W. and William's son, Richard "R.H." Gillespie.

In 1892, the Gillespies began to publish every day, a move that prompted derisive comments from those who doubted Stamford could support a daily newspaper. The skeptics were proved wrong, however. Not only did the paper succeed, it flourished. City Editor Robert Whittaker, a fervent believer in local news, was a key player in the growth of the daily edition. At first, Whittaker did almost all the local reporting himself. But he continued writing even after the staff was enlarged. He also lectured and sat on important local panels such as the Board of Trade, the Common Council, the School Committee and the Republican Town Committee. He left the paper in 1921 to become postmaster.

R.H. Gillespie died in 1911. He was succeeded by his son, Richard Jr., who followed the tradition of covering local news, thus assuring the steady growth of the paper's circulation as the community grew and prospered.

When Richard Jr. died in 1941, his brother, Schuyler, took over briefly as publisher. After his death the same year, Kingsley A. Gillespie, another of R.H.'s sons, was put in charge. It was during Kingsley's three decades of stewardship that the newspaper entered the modern era. The name was officially changed from *The Stamford Advocate* to *The Advocate* in 1974, an acknowledgement of the paper's growing influence beyond the city borders. A new press was purchased and the production technology was updated. Computer terminals gradually replaced typewriters in the newsroom. Another newspaper, *Greenwich Time,* was acquired. The company also bought (and later sold) an interest in the Stamford radio station, WSTC.

But the most dramatic change resulted from Kingsley's decision in 1977 to sell *The Advocate* and *Greenwich Time* to the Los Angeles-based Times Mirror Co. One of the nation's leading communications conglomerates, Times Mirror owns *The Los Angeles Times, The Hartford Courant, Newsday, The Baltimore Sun* and *The Morning Call* of Allentown, Pa. The company also owns several television stations, and magazine and book publishing firms.

Arthur Helms, now *The Advocate's* editorial page editor, was city editor in 1978. He has worked at the newspaper for most of the last two decades and remembers those days of change. "*The Advocate* went from being a family-owned newspaper —in effect, a one-man show — to a corporation-owned paper without much warning," Helms recalls. "Naturally there was trepidation in the newsroom, but it dissipated quickly. It was really a positive and energizing change. Our horizon expanded."

After a brief transition period, Times Mirror appointed Jay Shaw as publisher of *The Advocate* and *Greenwich Time.* He was followed by Steven

In 1981, The Advocate moved its offices and production plant to a modern facility on the corner of Tresser and Washington Boulevards.

Isenberg in 1983. William J. Rowe was named publisher in 1986.

One of *The Advocate's* finest moments came in 1978, when staff writer Anthony Dolan was awarded a Pulitzer Prize for his previous year's reporting on corruption in local government. In recent years, *The Advocate* has been honored by many professional organizations, including the Associated Press, United Press International, the Deadline Club, the Society of Silurians and the Connecticut Chapter of Sigma Delta Chi. In 1989, the New England Newspaper Association selected *The Advocate* as best newspaper in New England in its circulation category.

For many decades, *The Advocate's* editorial and production offices were in a building on Atlantic Street. The building, with its handsome neoclassical facade, still graces the block. In 1981, *The Advocate* moved to a new facility at the corner of Tresser and Washington Boulevards. It's worth noting that when *The Advocate* began the construction of its new headquarters, a magnificent copper beech tree stood on the building site. Instead of uprooting the stately tree, the publisher made certain the new building was designed around it. That copper beech remains standing today, a living testament to the newspaper's commitment to the community.

The Ferguson Library:
110 Years Young and Still Growing

Ernest A. DiMattia Jr.

THE BRASS PLAQUE in the foyer of the Ferguson Library's central building reads, "In honor of John Day Ferguson, 1832–1877, through whose efforts this library was founded. A man of sterling character, of endearing qualities and of fine culture. A citizen who gladly donated to the best interests of his town, his time, his energy and his high intelligence." Little did he know that his bequest of $10,000 to finance a public library, given on the condition that the community in turn donate $25,000, would establish an institution that itself would also be of "sterling character, endearing qualities and fine culture, gladly devoted to the best interests of the city" it serves.

And so it was in 1877 that the concept of a public library for Stamford was created. One year later, an editorial in *The Advocate* referring to Ferguson's gift would note that it "will furnish Stamford with the finest library in the state, if we except that of Yale College." However, it would not be until the beginning of 1880 that the first board would meet to name the library after John Day Ferguson, and several months later that the legislature of the State of Connecticut would formally incorporate the library "for the use of the people of Stamford."

The Ferguson Library opened its doors to the public in January 1882, at its initial location in Dr. Payne's building on Atlantic Street in downtown Stamford. Several years later in 1889, it would make its first move to the Geib property to occupy a majestic home, also on Atlantic Street near the Advocate building. In the late 1880's the library boasted a collection of 6,000 volumes and an annual circulation of more than 13,000. Library regulations at that time included a fee of $1.50 per year for the privilege of borrowing books and free use of the reading room at all times.

It was even reported that afternoon hours were "exclusively for ladies." It would not be until 1909 that the primary support of The Ferguson Library would be provided by the city itself through its tax revenues, and that public services, including the loan of books, would become totally free.

The Ferguson Library would make its second and final move in 1911 to its new facilities at the corner of Broad and Bedford Streets, several blocks from its Atlantic Street house, where it remains to this day as a reminder of a Stamford architecture that once was.

Over the years, Ferguson's main building was enlarged and enhanced in keeping with the growth and development of its collections, services and use. In 1930, after almost twenty years of operation, an expansion occurred which would house the library's children's, business and technical materials and services. Three decades later, the central building was doubled in size to 40,000 square feet through the addition of a new wing at the rear of the building, replacing a small park used by downtown strollers. With the establishment of a side entrance on Bedford Street, Ferguson was demonstrating its need to respond positively to the use and demands being made on it.

In 1982, just 100 years after it first opened its doors to the public, the biggest expansion and renovation project in the library's history was completed and dedicated. Restoring the old 1911 facade and adding a new four-story marble and glass structure, Ferguson was transformed into a

In 1911, The Ferguson Library moved to the neo-Federal-style structure which remains its home today.

modern 100,000 square foot library building, with furnishings and an ambience that would rival any other public facility.

As it grew in response to community needs, The Ferguson Library started a program of user outreach that began with the initiation of bookmobile service in 1940, continued with the acquisition of the Weed Memorial Branch in 1954 and the Turn of River Branch in 1967, and culminated in the establishment of the South End Community Center Branch in 1968.

With the purchase of its first vehicle some fifty years ago, The Ferguson Library was among the pioneers in bookmobile service. The 1940 version carried books on exterior shelves on both sides of a truck. The volumes were protected by large glass covers that were raised to allow borrowers to peruse the shelves. This vehicle, as would its successors, made stops in various parts of the city and reached out to potential users who, for one reason or another, could not use the central building.

Over the years, bookmobile service increased in size and popularity, as well as in the sophistication of the vehicles being acquired. The second

bookmobile was a small trailer pulled by a truck, while the third found an even larger truck/trailer combination being put into service. The first of the self-contained large truck type vehicles took to the road in 1975, and was followed by the present, modern, 39-foot version which was put into service in 1987. In 1989, a smaller, sixth edition was purchased as a multi-purpose van in order to provide a suitable alternative when the main vehicle is off the road, or when special mobile service must be made available.

The donation of the Weed Memorial branch in 1954 added a new dimension to library services in Stamford with the establishment of the first neighborhood facility in the Springdale section of the city. Dating back to 1810, the building was originally constructed as a home, and therefore had to undergo some renovation before a library could be operational. This was accomplished through a broad-based community effort, which was a tribute both to the donor, Jennie Weed, and to the concept of having a local library.

In a somewhat dissimilar manner, the Turn of River Branch was a major community effort through the raising of funds to purchase an abandoned church and parsonage on High Ridge Road. The buildings were turned over to the library board to be used to serve Turn of River and North Stamford residents and business users. Four portable classrooms were added in 1980 and were designed to provide a separate children's area and meeting/program room. Little did the local organizers realize that the Turn of River facility would become the most heavily used branch library facility in the entire State of Connecticut, with the circulation of all items reaching almost one quarter million annually.

Completing Ferguson's outreach was the creation of a branch facility in the South End Community Center. Starting first as a one room library in 1968, and then doubling its size some two decades later, the South End Branch has become an important element in the vast array of services offered by Ferguson.

Along with the establishment and growth of library facilities over the past century has been the development of an extensive and diverse collection of books and other related materials for public use. Starting with the acquisition of hardbound books in the 19th century, Ferguson has maintained its philosophy of purchasing the kinds of print and non-print materials that meet and fulfill the demands of its users. Such items as magazines, newspapers, phonograph recordings, 16mm films, paperback books, microfilm, audio

cassettes, art reproductions, compact discs, sculpture and video cassettes have, over the years, also been acquired as they became available and popular.

In the area of automation, Ferguson was, in the early 1970's, one of the first public libraries to join a national bibliographic database, originally established for college libraries, in order to facilitate the cataloging of materials and the location of books for purposes of interlibrary loan. The introduction of an internal, online circulation system some two decades ago also helped the entire public library field in pioneering the application of computers in the improvement and extension of public service. Automation has become so accepted by library users that the traditional card catalog has been replaced by modern keyboard terminals. Those with personal computers at home can now remotely access the full catalog, obtaining information on more than one-half million print and non-print items in the entire collection. In addition, a recently installed data radio system allows bookmobile users to be on-line, as well, and to find the location and status of any item. Such interactivity is just the beginning of the computer capabilities that will allow Ferguson to offer its clientele more access to more information on a 24-hour per day, seven-day per week basis.

A satellite area of service and activity has been

Comfortable chairs and pleasant surroundings encourage readers in the periodicals room of the Library.

Whether for research or pure enjoyment, The Ferguson Library's facilities attract heavy public use.

in the programs and exhibits the library has to offer. Ferguson has long been noted for the diversity and extent of its programming for young and old alike, whether in its story hours for toddlers, book discussion groups for nursing home residents or film showings for all ages. Both internally and externally, programs have traditionally played a vital role in the array of services provided to the community. With the opening of the new main library in the early 1980's, several areas were set aside for the mounting of exhibits and displays. This newest programming effort has proved very successful and popular.

One of the exceptional strengths of Ferguson as a public library has been its interaction with the community. Through the use of special events, programs, exhibits and publications, the library has reached out to its various constituencies to bring specialities and services to bear as directly as possible. As a result of this long practice, Ferguson has been successful in impacting and influencing many educational, cultural, governmental and social elements within Stamford, and to insure broader knowledge and utilization of its services, collections, programs and facilities. Indeed, this effort began early in the library's history

and has, over the years, proved extremely beneficial to all concerned.

And yet, with all of the diversified services, multifaceted collections, varied programming and vast technological advances that have made Ferguson the renowned public library it is today, the one factor that has caused all this to happen is embodied in the wonderful array of people who have influenced and guided the library during its century plus of growth and development.

Whether it be the users of the library requesting more and more in services, materials and programs, the members of the Board of Trustees setting policy and seeking support, the officials in city government recognizing the library's importance and allocating as much public funding as possible, the Citizen Advisors, Friends and other supporters providing expertise to help make possible various projects and programs, the volunteers giving their time and talent, or the members of the staff taking professionally and seriously their responsibilities to insure excellence in public library service, it has been people dedicated to a community and to an institution that have made Ferguson such an outstanding public library.

How This Book Came About

Barry Hoffman

Managing Editor, The Advocate

THIS BOOK IS BASED on the straightforward notion that people ought to be aware of their surroundings. Such awareness makes life more interesting, lends a certain sense of continuity and helps us see events in the proper perspective.

Human nature being what it is, however, we often find ourselves taking for granted that which has become comfortable and familiar.

One purpose of this book is to remind us that Stamford actually is a very beautiful city — an uncommonly rare mixture of corporate, residential and maritime neighborhoods rubbing shoulders on a patch of real estate less than 40 miles square.

The cover photograph really tells the story: Stamford is a city of boats, buildings and homes. It most certainly is not just another homogenous suburban bedroom community. It's a wonderful collection of communities, each with its own distinct flavor and accent. Too often, in our haste to get through the daily chores, we forget that we live in a unique place.

Ideally, this book will allow the reader to view Stamford through fresh eyes. We hope the brief history we've written will engender a feeling of connection with Stamford's past. And perhaps, knowing where the city came from will give the reader a better notion of where the city is going.

The other purpose of this book is to celebrate Stamford's 350th anniversary. In this regard, we are carrying on a sturdy tradition at *The Advocate*, which printed special publications to mark the city's 250th and 300th anniversaries. We weren't about to let that tradition slip — to forget such a birthday would be unforgivable.

Fortunately, we were able to glean much from the experience of our sister newspaper, *Greenwich Time*, which published a similar book last year to mark Greenwich's 350th anniversary. William J. Rowe, publisher of *The Advocate* and *Greenwich Time*, decided back in 1989 that both books should be highly readable and gorgeous to look at. Both books would contain lively stories about real people, the purpose being to excite the imagination.

Neither book would be a scholarly tome or dry history.

To ensure that both books would be genuinely beautiful to behold, the services of noted photographer William Hubbell were secured. Rowe had seen some of Hubbell's previous work in a handsome book entitled *Connecticut* and was convinced he could capture on film the special magic of our area. Both books are testaments to Hubbell's extraordinary vision.

For the Stamford book, art historian Renee Kahn was assigned the task of finding old photographs, engravings and illustrations to show the community in its early years. All archival material for the book was gathered from the collections of the Stamford Historical Society and the Historic Neighborhood Preservation Program.

Don Russell, *The Advocate's* local columnist, and Mike Barlow, *The Advocate's* executive news editor, were assigned to research and write a compact yet vivid history of the city. Ernest DiMattia, president and executive director of the Ferguson Library, was asked to write a brief history of that venerable institution.

Last but certainly not least, syndicated columnist, author and television talk show host William F. Buckley Jr. was asked to write a reminiscence about Stamford, where he has made his home for many years. As one would expect, Buckley's essay is elegant, erudite and thoroughly entertaining.

Robert Atwan served as the book's consulting editor.

To all of the above, we offer thanks and congratulations for a job well done.

Financing for the book was made possible by a grant from *The Advocate* and a matching grant from the Times Mirror Co. The Ferguson Library, through a grant from The Max and Victoria Dreyfus Foundation, also participated in this project. Profits from the book will benefit the Ferguson Library Foundation.

We also would like to express our thanks to the Stamford Historical Society for the generous use of its photo archives. We are especially grateful for the assistance of Lois R. Dater, Curator Emeritus of the Society. In the months before her death in January, 1991, she spent many hours helping the authors of this book locate old photographs and other important research materials. We also wish to sincerely thank Dr. Estelle Feinstein, Professor Emeritus of History at the University of Connecticut, and Ronald Marcus, Chief Librarian of the Stamford Historical Society, for their advice and expert assistance.

Additionally, we would like to thank the Yaraghi family, owners of the former Stamford Fidelity Bank building on Atlantic Street; the Ferguson Library and its superb staff; and Donna Callighan, Beth Cox, Carol Lang, Doreen Park, Sean Konecky, Hannah Lerner and Jim Wasserman, all of whom performed service above and beyond the call of duty to see this project through successfully.

And of course, we want to thank the people of Stamford, who have made this city a great place in which to work and live.

A Selected Bibliography

The Advocate. *Picturesque Stamford.* Published by Gillespie Brothers, Inc. (1892).

The Advocate. *Stamford Advocate Tercentenary Edition.* Published by Gillespie Brothers, Inc. (1941).

Rosemary H. Burns. *Springdale Remembered: The History of a Section of Stamford, Connecticut.* Published by the Stamford Historical Society (1982).

Estelle Feinstein. *Stamford From Puritan to Patriot.* Published by the Stamford Bicentennial Committee (1976).

Estelle Feinstein and Joyce S. Pendery. *Stamford: An Illustrated History.* Produced in cooperation with the Stamford Historical Society by Windsor Publications Inc., Woodland Hills, California (1984).

Herbert F. Sherwood. *The Story of Stamford.* Published by the States History Company (1930).

Stamford Bicentennial Committee. *Stamford Past and Present .* The Commemorative Publication of the Stamford Bicentennial Committee.